IF I DON'T KNOW

WENDY COPE

If I Don't Know

——

ff

faber and faber

Faber and Faber Limited

Photoset by Wilmaset Ltd, Birkenhead
Printed in Italy

All rights reserved
© Wendy Cope, 2001

The right of Wendy Cope to be identified as author
of this work has been asserted in accordance with Section 77
of the Copyright, Designs and Patents Act 1988

A CIP record for this book
is available from the British Library

ISBN 0–571–20767–7 (cased)
0–571–20955–6 (pbk)
0–571–21052–x (limited edition)

2 4 6 8 10 9 7 5 3 1

To LM
with love and thanks

Contents

Acknowledgements

Some of these poems first appeared in *Areté*, *The Author*, *The Daily Telegraph*, *The Dark Horse*, *The Faber Book of Christmas*, *For John Clare* (The John Clare Society), *Independent on Sunday*, *Last Words* (Salisbury Festival/Picador), *Mslexia*, *New Writing 7* (British Council/Vintage), *The Observer*, *101 Poems That Could Save Your Life* (HarperCollins), *Orbis*, *New Canterbury Tales* (Canterbury Festival), *Poetry Review*, *The Poet's View* (Headland), *Second Shift*, *Times Educational Supplement*, *Writing on the Wall* (Weidenfeld and Nicolson).

Five of them were published as a limited edition, *Being Boring* (Aralia Press, USA). Clarion Publishing produced a limited edition of 'The Squirrel and the Crow', with line drawings by John Vernon Lord. 'Poem from a Colour Chart of House Paints' first appeared as a Priapus Press booklet.

'The Teacher's Tale' is one of a number of stories, by various authors, commissioned by the Canterbury Festival to mark the 600th anniversary of the death of Geoffrey Chaucer.

'Elegy for the Northern Wey' was commissioned by Dr Trevor Weston for The Northern Wey Trust. Dr Weston also commissioned 'By the Round Pond', as part of a series of poems linked to paintings by Peter Rodulfo.

I owe the idea for the form of 'The Lyric Poet' to Edwin Morgan, who has used it in several poems.

'The Christmas Life' has been set to music by Martin Read. His setting, for soprano and alto voices and piano, is published by Banks of York. A setting of 'He Tells Her', by the same composer (for soprano, clarinet in A, viola and violoncello), is available from Fand Music Press.

My thanks to the founder, trustees and staff of Hawthornden Castle International Retreat for Writers, where I stayed for a month in 1993 and wrote four of these poems.

I

By the Round Pond

You watch yourself. You watch the watcher too –
A ghostly figure on the garden wall.
And one of you is her, and one is you,
If either one of you exists at all.

How strange to be the one behind a face,
To have a name and know that it is yours,
To be in this particular green place,
To see a snail advance, to see it pause.

You sit quite still and wonder when you'll go.
It could be now. Or now. Or now. You stay.
Who's making up the plot? You'll never know.
Minute after minute swims away.

The Christmas Life

'If you don't have a real tree, you don't bring the Christmas life
into the house.'

Josephine Mackinnon, aged 8

Bring in a tree, a young Norwegian spruce,
Bring hyacinths that rooted in the cold.
Bring winter jasmine as its buds unfold –
Bring the Christmas life into this house.

Bring red and green and gold, bring things that shine,
Bring candlesticks and music, food and wine.
Bring in your memories of Christmas past.
Bring in your tears for all that you have lost.

Bring in the shepherd boy, the ox and ass,
Bring in the stillness of an icy night,
Bring in a birth, of hope and love and light.
Bring the Christmas life into this house.

30th December

At first I'm startled by the sound of bicycles
Above my head. And then I see them, two swans
Flying in to their runway behind the reeds.

The bridge is slippery, the grass so sodden
That water seeps into my shoes. But now
The sun has come out and everything is calm
And beautiful as the end of a hangover.

Christmas was a muddle
Of turkey bones and muted quarrelling.

The visitors have left.
Solitary walkers smile and tell each other
That the day is wonderful.

If only this could be Christmas now –
These shining meadows,
The hum of huge wings in the sky.

If I Don't Know
(for Louise Kerr)

If I don't know how to be thankful enough
for the clusters of white blossom

on our mock orange, which has grown tall
and graceful, come into its own

like a new star just out of ballet school,
and if I don't know what to do

about those spires of sky-blue delphinium,
then what about the way they look together?

And what about the roses, or just one of them –
that solid pinky-peachy bloom

that hollows towards its heart? Outrageous.
I could crush it to bits.

A photograph? A dance to summer?
I sit on the swing and cry.

The rose. The gardenful. The evening light.
It's nine o'clock and I can still see everything.

[6]

Haiku: Looking Out of the Back Bedroom Window without My Glasses

What's that amazing
new lemon-yellow flower?
Oh yes, a football.

Idyll

(after U. A. Fanthorpe)

We'll be in our garden on a summer evening,
Eating pasta, drinking white wine.

We won't talk all the time. I'll sit back,
Contemplating shadows on the red-brick path,

And marvel at the way it all turned out.
That yellow begonia. Our gabled house.

Later we'll stroll through Kingsgate Park.
My leg won't hurt, and we'll go home the long way.

Asked to imagine heaven, I see us there,
The way we have been, the way we sometimes are.

Being Boring

'May you live in interesting times.' Chinese curse

If you ask me 'What's new?', I have nothing to say
Except that the garden is growing.
I had a slight cold but it's better today.
I'm content with the way things are going.
Yes, he is the same as he usually is,
Still eating and sleeping and snoring.
I get on with my work. He gets on with his.
I know this is all very boring.

There was drama enough in my turbulent past:
Tears and passion – I've used up a tankful.
No news is good news, and long may it last.
If nothing much happens, I'm thankful.
A happier cabbage you never did see,
My vegetable spirits are soaring.
If you're after excitement, steer well clear of me.
I want to go on being boring.

I don't go to parties. Well, what are they for,
If you don't need to find a new lover?
You drink and you listen and drink a bit more
And you take the next day to recover.
Someone to stay home with was all my desire
And, now that I've found a safe mooring,
I've just one ambition in life: I aspire
To go on and on being boring.

Fireworks Poems

(commissioned by the Salisbury Festival
to be displayed in fireworks)

I

Faster and faster,
They vanish into darkness:
Our years together.

II

Write it in fire across the night:
Some men are more or less all right.

Timekeeping

Late home for supper,
He mustn't seem drunk.
'The pob cluck', he begins,
And knows he is sunk.

Song

My love got in the car
And sat on my banana,
My unobserved banana
And my organic crisps.

We spoke of life and love,
His rump on my banana,
My hidden, soft banana
And my forgotten crisps.

He kissed me more than once
As he sat on that banana,
That newly-squashed banana
And those endangered crisps.

We looked up at the stars –
Beneath him, my banana,
My saved-from-lunch banana
And my delicious crisps.

At last I dropped him off
And noticed the banana –
Alas, a ruined banana
And sadly damaged crisps.

You'd think he would have felt
A fairly large banana
And, if not the banana,
The lumpy bag of crisps.

But he's the kind of man
Who'll sit on a banana
For hours. Watch your banana
And guard your bag of crisps.

He waved goodbye and smiled,
Benign as a banana.
'I love you, daft banana,'
Said I, and ate the crisps.

On a Train

The book I've been reading
rests on my knee. You sleep.

It's beautiful out there –
fields, little lakes and winter trees
in February sunlight,
every car park a shining mosaic.

Long, radiant minutes,
your hand in my hand,
still warm, still warm.

Present

On the flyleaf
of my confirmation present:
'To Wendy with love
from Nanna. Psalm 98.'

I looked it up, eventually –
Cantate Domino.
I knew the first two verses
and skimmed the rest.

Thirty-five years afterwards,
at evensong on Day 19
the choir sings Nanna's psalm.
At last, I pay attention

to the words she chose.
O sing unto the Lord
a new song. Nanna,
it is just what I wanted.

Postcards

(commissioned for broadcast by BBC World Service)

At first I sent you a postcard
From every city I went to.
Grüsse aus Bath, aus Birmingham,
Aus Rotterdam, aus Tel Aviv.
Mit Liebe. Cards from you arrived
In English, with many commas.
Hope, you're fine and still alive,
Says one from Hong Kong. By that time
We weren't writing quite as often.

Now we're nearly nine years away
From the lake and the blue mountains,
And the room with the balcony,
But the heat and light of those days
Can reach this far from time to time.
Your latest was from Senegal,
Mine from Helsinki. I don't know
If we'll meet again. Be happy.
If you hear this, send a postcard.

Sonnet of '68

The uproar's over, and the calls to fight
For freedom, the Utopian fantasies.
We took a fairground ride to Paradise
And afterwards there's nothing more, goodnight.

The fire burnt out. The veterans, turning grey,
Make legends of the beautiful, wild past.
These will stay with us till we breathe our last:
The red flag and the photograph of Che.

So many speeches. There's a silence now.
Each of us walks along the city street
Alone, concerned about his daily bread.

We overreached ourselves a little bit.
Euphoria didn't suit us anyhow.
Those who did not outgrow it – they are dead.

Translated from the German of Harry Oberländer

A Word before Sleep

(after Marina Tsvetayeva)

Life tells us lies, inimitably,
Beyond all expectations, outdoing other liars.
You know, when all your veins are trembling,
You recognise it – life!

It is as if you're lying in a field of rye,
In ringing blueness, falling heat (and so what if it's lies
You're lying in), the sound of bees through
   honeysuckle.
Rejoice. You have been called.

No, don't reproach me, my dear friend –
Our souls are easily bewitched,
Already, now, my head is entering a dream.
Why did you sing?

Your quietnesses are a clean, white book,
Your 'yesses', savage clay.
I bend my head towards them, quietly.
The palm of my hand – life.

Note: Tsvetayeva composed her poem in June 1922 after reading
Boris Pasternak's book *My Sister Life*. I made use of a literal
translation from the Russian by Gerard Smith.

After Prague

(Marina Tsvetayeva)

He went. You said
you didn't want to live –

but there were other cities,
sixteen years,

before you reached the end,
alone in Yelabuga.

Hope is a long leash,
drawn in slowly.

The Sitter

(Vanessa Bell, *Nude*, c.1922–3, Tate Britain)

Depressed and disagreeable and fat –
That's how she saw me. It was all she saw.
Around her, yes, I may have looked like that.
She hardly spoke. She thought I was a bore.
Beneath her gaze I couldn't help but slouch.
She made me feel ashamed. My face went red.
I'd rather have been posing on a couch
For some old rake who wanted me in bed.
Some people made me smile, they made me shine,
They made me beautiful. But they're all gone,
Those friends, the way they saw this face of mine,
And her contempt for me is what lives on.
Admired, well-bred, artistic Mrs Bell,
I hope you're looking hideous in Hell.

Les Vacances

(Walter Richard Sickert, *Bathers, Dieppe*, 1902,
Walker Art Gallery, Liverpool)

Maman et Papa au bord de la mer.
Aujourd'hui il fait beau. I remember it well.
Voilà Armand, in the corner down there,
With Maman et Papa au bord de la mer!
Oh, bored, c'est le mot. I tear out the hair
As we limp through ce livre avec Mademoiselle.
Maman et Papa au bord de la mer.
Il fait beau. I remember it only too well.

Dead Sheep Poem

This morning we saw sheepskin rugs
Outside the craft shop in the village.

Now we've found one on the hillside,
Soft and creamy-white among the thistles,

Cushioning a rib-cage and a line
Of vertebrae, laid out like stepping-stones.

Nine feet away, the skull
And jawbone, clean as carved ivory.

Crows and maggots cleared off long ago –
The person with the notebook has arrived.

The Lyric Poet
(from a line by Heine)

```
I       ache
I               die
I   m               in
        he      l       l
I   ma      k e
        a           l ine
        ma      d
                i   l       l
        a
        ch  i   l           d
                    in
                    ne      ed
I   ma      k e
        a           l ine
        he
c   a       l       l ed
    m   e
        he
        he      l       d
    m   e
        he
                l i e       d
I   ma      k e
        a           l ine
        a           n
        ac  e   l ine
        che         e       r
```

Ich mache die kleinen Lieder

[23]

A Mystery

People say, 'What are you doing these days? What are
   you working on?'
I think for a moment or two.

The question interests me. What am I doing these
   days?
How odd that I haven't a clue.

Right now, of course, I'm working on this poem,
With just a few more lines to go.

But tomorrow someone will ask me, 'What are you up
   to these days? What are you working on?'
And I still won't know.

Reading Berryman's *Dream Songs*
at the Writers' Retreat

Wendy went a-swimming. It was dreadful.
One small boy careless under her did surface
and did butt her on the chin.
Of space to swim was hardly any,
fearful shoutings, bodies from the springboard
splash when jumping in.

Why no school? cried agey Wendy
to herself, not loud. Why little beggars
swimming into me on Friday afternoon?
Why not in cage, learn tables?
Out and dress and buy bananas.
Yogurt? No. Need spoon.

Once more to Hawthornden through Scottish fog.
Back up to poet's lair and sit on bed.
Is you bored, Bones, all by youzeself
wif read and write and bein' deep?
Not for a moment.
Now, a little sleep.

The Squirrel and the Crow

Each day I take a morning walk
Above the River Esk,
In preparation for long hours
Of writing at my desk.

And when the healthy Scottish air
Has cleared my sleepy head,
I climb three flights of stairs, collapse
Exhausted on my bed,

Pick up the daily paper, try
To solve some crossword clues,
And when I can't do any more,
Find notebook, summon Muse.

But she will not co-operate,
That wayward Muse of mine.
She seems to mutter, 'Have a heart,
It's only ten past nine.'

Though other writers all around
Type, type and do not shirk,
This maxim saves me from depression:
Reading books is work.

I pick up Edward Thomas,
Collected, fairly slim,
And read it for an hour and wish
That I could write like him.

Next day I walk with glasses on
To see what I can find
Of natural things that may, perhaps,
Improve my urban mind.

I notice tiny bugle flowers,
Each one a bright blue star
(Although, until I look them up,
I don't know what they are).

Red campion, pink purslane – riches
Everywhere I look.
Wood-sorrel, greater stitchwort (all
Are in The Oxford Book).

I wander on until I see
Before me on the track –
This will be something horrible –
Two lumps, one grey, one black.

And, drawing closer, find a squirrel
Who has lost his head
Or hers. The other is a crow,
And this, too, is stone dead.

What happened? Here's my first attempt
At answering the question:
The crow bit off the squirrel's head
And died of indigestion.

I leave a note for Roy next door
(We aren't allowed to talk

Till dinner-time) and head it HORROR
ON THE CASTLE WALK!

And he, a trained zoologist,
Explains it was not so:
A squirrel is too big to be
Beheaded by a crow.

Post-mortem on the squirrel: Roy
Concludes that someone shot it.
As for the crow, we do not know
What quirk of fortune got it.

The absence of the squirrel's head
Remains a mystery.
My quiet, lovely nature poem –
That was not to be.

Men in prison: one sees stars,
Another, only mud.
Poets walking: some find solace,
Others, guts and blood.

John Clare

John Clare, I cried last night
For you – your grass-green coat,
Your oddness, others' spite,
Your fame, enjoyed and lost,
Your gift, and what it cost.

Awake in the early hours,
I heard you with my eyes,
Carolling woods and showers.
As if a songbird's throat
Could utter words, you wrote.

I listened late and long –
Each clear, true, loving note
Placed justly in its song.
Sometimes for sheer delight,
John Clare, I cried last night.

An Ending

Don't want to leave this place,
This time, this happiness:
Loud water, muddy tracks,
Trees rooted in pink rocks,
Our lush, steep-sided glen,
Friends I may see again
But certainly not here,
Not in this world we were.

For one short month our home,
This world will soon be gone.
Though those unruly birds
Still chirp and caw, though woods
Breathe on, if we return,
Each one of us alone,
It will not be to find
What we now leave behind.

Out there beyond the gates,
We'll take our random routes
Through time and space. How far,
How long, we can't be sure.
We'll have to say goodbye
To more than this one day.
Tomorrow, we rehearse,
And quietly leave this place.

Poem from a Colour Chart of House Paints

Limeglow of leaves –
elf, sapling
in Elysian green,
she's jitterbugging
in the forest.
She is froth, the tang
of julep, capering
among the ferns.

Passion, the firedance
of her fantasy,
fireglow of poppy
and corona, ember.
Casanova, peerless
demon, jester!
She burns, a firefly,
Apollo's geisha.

Her sandgold hair,
spun silk kimono,
melon and lemon sorbet
on the balcony,
white wine, gardenias.
That honeysuckle year –
if he could ransom
one sunlit day!

Indigo seascape –
Melissa in cool,

blue moonshade.
Harebell, naiad,
exotic ballerina,
she commands the bay,
the midnight swell,
the surf, pale gossamer.

Autumnal in brogues,
beige twinset, russet
tweeds, she takes
coffee at eleven,
sherry at noon –
dreams of Tarragona,
castanets, a man
who called her Sheba.

Her mood
is violet, nocturnal.
Aubrietia, phlox,
wisteria delight her
more than roses.
Solitude, a purple
robe, a last
long hazy evening.

Greek Island Triolets

1 *Entomological*

This fly believes I'm dead.
I cannot lift a finger.
He buzzes round my head.
This fly believes I'm dead –
A body on a bed,
Safe place for him to linger.
This fly believes I'm dead.
I cannot lift a finger.

2 *Sartorial*

Why did I buy this Marks and Spencer's T-shirt
And, having done so, fail to take it back?
An average English-frump-beside-the-sea-shirt –
Why did I buy this Marks and Spencer's T-shirt?
I needed something ace. This is a B-shirt,
Fit only to be worn beneath a mac.
Why did I buy this Marks and Spencer's T-shirt?
Shall I wash it once and take it back?

3 Arboreal

We hugged a tree last night
And all of us enjoyed it.
Ecstatic, by moonlight,
We hugged a tree last night.
Trees can't put up a fight –
That oak could not avoid it.
We hugged it good and tight –
I hope the tree enjoyed it.

The Ted Williams Villanelle
(for Ari Badaines)

Don't let anybody mess with your swing.'
Ted Williams, baseball player

Watch the ball and do your thing.
This is the moment. Here's your chance.
Don't let anybody mess with your swing.

It's time to shine. You're in the ring.
Step forward, adopt a winning stance,
Watch the ball and do your thing,

And while that ball is taking wing,
Run, without a backward glance.
Don't let anybody mess with your swing.

Don't let envious bastards bring
You down. Ignore the sneers, the can'ts.
Watch the ball and do your thing.

Sing out, if you want to sing.
Jump up, when you long to dance.
Don't let anybody mess with your swing.

Enjoy your talents. Have your fling.
The seasons change. The years advance.
Watch the ball and do your thing,
And don't let anybody mess with your swing.

He Tells Her

He tells her that the Earth is flat –
He knows the facts, and that is that.
In altercations fierce and long
She tries her best to prove him wrong.
But he has learned to argue well.
He calls her arguments unsound
And often asks her not to yell.
She cannot win. He stands his ground.

The planet goes on being round.

What I Think

All right, I'll tell you what I think.
I'll tell you more than once or twice:
You really ought to see a shrink.

Your psyche isn't in the pink,
Your home is not a paradise,
All right? I'll tell you what I think:

Though you get by, with friends and drink
And rhymed despair (our common vice),
You really ought to see a shrink.

Of course, it's scary. You won't sink.
You'll cry a lot. It's worth the price,
All right? I'll tell you what I think:

I've wasted breath, I'm wasting ink.
I'm smothering you with advice.
You really ought to see a shrink.

I want you happy, stupid gink.
I'm here for you till Hell is ice.
All right, I've told you what I think.
For God's sake, go and see a shrink.

The Sorrow of Socks

Some socks are loners –
They can't live in pairs.
On washdays they've shown us
They want to be loners.
They puzzle their owners,
They hide in dark lairs.
Some socks are loners –
They won't live in pairs.

The Stickleback Song

'Someone should see to the dead stickleback.'
School inspector to London headteacher

A team of inspectors came round here today,
They looked at our school and pronounced it OK.
We've no need to worry, we shan't get the sack,
But someone should see to the dead stickleback.
Dead stickleback, dead stickleback,
But someone should see to the dead stickleback.

Well, we've got some gerbils, all thumping their tails,
And we've got a tankful of live water-snails,
But there's one little creature we certainly lack –
We haven't a quick or a dead stickleback.
Dead stickleback, dead stickleback,
We haven't a quick or a dead stickleback.

Oh was it a spectre the inspector saw,
The ghost of some poor classroom pet who's no more?
And will it be friendly or will it attack?
We're living in fear of the dead stickleback.
Dead stickleback, dead stickleback,
We're living in fear of the dead stickleback.

Or perhaps there's a moral to this little song:
Inspectors work hard and their hours are too long.
When they overdo it, their minds start to crack
And they begin seeing the dead stickleback.
Dead stickleback, dead stickleback,
And they begin seeing the dead stickleback.

[39]

Now all you young teachers, so eager and good,
You won't lose your wits for a few years, touch wood.
But take off as fast as a hare on the track
The day you encounter the dead stickleback.
Dead stickleback, dead stickleback,
The day you encounter the dead stickleback.

Stress

(for Henry Thompson, but not about him)

He would refuse to put the refuse out.
The contents of the bin would start to smell.
How could she be content? That idle lout
Would drive the tamest woman to rebel.
And, now that she's a rebel, he frequents
The pub for frequent drink-ups with a mate
Who nods a lot whenever he presents
His present life at home as far from great.
The drinking makes his conduct even worse
And she conducts herself like some poor soul
In torment. She torments her friends with verse,
Her protest poems – dreadful, on the whole.
We daren't protest. Why risk an upset when
She's so upset already? I blame men.

A Hampshire Disaster

'Shock was the emotion of most.'
Hampshire Chronicle, 13 May 1994

When fire engulfed the headquarters
Of the Royal Winchester Golf Club
In the early hours of Wednesday morning,
Shock was the emotion of most.

But fear had been the emotion
Of some who saw the flames, and admiration
For the courage and skill of the firefighters
Was another emotion felt.

At the loss of so much history –
Cups, trophies, and honours boards –
Sadness is now the emotion
Of many Winchester golfers.

Stoical resignation was the emotion
Of the club captain, as he told the *Chronicle*
'The next procedure will be to sort out the insurance.
Life must go on.'

A Poem on the Theme of Humour
(for Gavin Ewart)

'Poems can be in any style and on any theme (except humour).'
Rules for the Bard of the Year competition 1994

Dear Organisers of Bard of the Year,

Suppose I were to write a completely solemn,
    joke-free and unamusing poem
And to send it in with my £3 entry fee,
And suppose the subject of that poem were humour in
    poetry,
Would you accept it?

There are serious things I want to say on this subject,
Such as how absolutely right you were to make that
    rule,
Because, if humour is allowed into a poem,
People may laugh and enjoy it,
Which gives the poet an unfair advantage.

I trust that the supervisor of the panel of judges,
    Dannie Abse,
('immediate past President of The Poetry Society and
    one of Britain's greatest poets'),
Will be rigorous in disqualifying any poem
That raises so much as a smile.

What a good idea to have a separate competition
Called 'Fun '94', with smaller prizes,

For those who write humorous poems!
It doesn't dilute your message to the reading public:
Real poetry is no fun at all.

A Reading

Everybody in this room is bored.
The poems drag, the voice and gestures irk.
He can't be interrupted or ignored.

Poor fools, we came here of our own accord
And some of us have paid to hear this jerk.
Everybody in the room is bored.

The silent cry goes up, 'How long, O Lord?'
But nobody will scream or go berserk.
He won't be interrupted or ignored

Or hit by eggs, or savaged by a horde
Of desperate people maddened by his work.
Everybody in the room is bored,

Except the poet. We are his reward,
Pretending to indulge his every quirk.
He won't be interrupted or ignored.

At last it's over. How we all applaud!
The poet thanks us with a modest smirk.
Everybody in the room was bored.
He wasn't interrupted or ignored.

How to Deal with the Press

She'll urge you to confide. Resist.
Be careful, courteous, and cool.
Never trust a journalist.

'We're off the record,' she'll insist.
If you believe her, you're a fool.
She'll urge you to confide. Resist.

Should you tell her who you've kissed,
You'll see it all in print, and you'll
Never trust a journalist

Again. The words are hers to twist,
And yours the risk of ridicule.
She'll urge you to confide. Resist.

'But X is nice,' the publicist
Will tell you. 'We were friends at school.'
Never trust a journalist,

Hostile, friendly, sober, pissed,
Male or female – that's the rule.
When tempted to confide, resist.
Never trust a journalist.

Traditional Prize County Pigs

1 *Wessex Saddleback*

A porcine aborigine,
He has no trace of foreign blood.
His ancestors were wild and free
British pigs in British mud.

He's a hardy, outdoor type,
Who's never heard of central heating.
He doesn't whine, he doesn't gripe
But, strong and silent, goes on eating.

2 *Oxfordshire Sandy and Black*

This piggy has a pedigree
That goes way back on Midlands farms.
If she could read her family tree,
She might design a coat of arms.

But she knows nothing of her line,
And lives like any other sow,
Taking care of little swine,
Imprisoned in the here and now.

3 *Cornish Lop-eared*

A fine white pig of goodly size,
He roots and gobbles from the ground

But when he tries to look around,
His lop ears droop across his eyes.

He doesn't know the world is big
And beautiful. He doesn't try
To wander. He's an easy pig,
Content to stay within his sty.

4 *Staffordshire Tamworth Red*

If you want to go away
On a summer holiday
And take your pig, make no mistake,
A Tamworth Red's the pig to take.

A pig whose skin is very fair
Will use up all your Ambre Solaire,
And need a hat, and cause concern,
But Tamworths very seldom burn.

5 *Orkney Boar*

If you should meet an Orkney Boar
A-roaming on an Orkney moor,
Beware. This savage little porker
May attack the English walker.

6 *Lincolnshire Curly Coat*

A pig of pigs. If free to scoff,
He'll seldom leave the feeding-trough,

Expanding till he's almost static
And procreation's problematic.

And that, I guess, is why the breed
By now is very rare indeed.

7 *Gloucestershire Old Spot*

Walking Rorschach tests, Old Spots
Have pure white skin with inky blots
But do not show an interest
In asking what the shapes suggest.

8 *Berkshire Prize Beauty*

Once the standard of perfection
By which other pigs were judged –
Lovely figure, great complexion
Even when her face was smudged.
Just imagine the dejection
As her rivals' owners trudged
To fatstock show and prize inspection,
Knowing she could not be budged.

9 *Old Glamorgan*

There isn't very much to write –
I only know he's large and white.

In Dorset in the days of old
There lived a pig whose hide was gold –
Friendly, beautiful, and charming,
Unsuitable for modern farming.
It can't be helped. The world moves on
And all the golden pigs are gone.

Elegy for the Northern Wey

(Polluted by an ammonia spillage, March 1999)

This is the moment:
March sunshine, trees almost bare,
everything stirring.

The birds know it too –
so loud, so full of themselves
this blissful morning.

White clouds. Tree-shadows.
The river. How clear it is,
how busy with life.

This is the moment
we can never get back to.
Look, a little frog.

Tulips

Months ago I dreamed of a tulip garden,
Planted, waited, watched for their first appearance,
Saw them bud, saw greenness give way to colours,
Just as I'd planned them.

Every day I wonder how long they'll be here.
Sad and fearing sadness as I admire them,
Knowing I must lose them, I almost wish them
Gone by tomorrow.

II

The Teacher's Tale

In London SE5 there lived a boy
Called Paul. He was his mother's pride and joy
When he was born in 1961 –
Best baby ever, Mrs Skinner's son.
He had a dad, too, living with his mum.
In this our Paul was luckier than some,
Since many dads of London SE5
Were not at home, though most were still alive.
Paul's dad, Gus Skinner, had a little shop
Where you could buy a dustbin or a mop,
An ironing board or other household stuff.
He wasn't rich but he had just enough
To keep his little family afloat
And buy his wife a decent winter coat
From time to time – not every other year
But one in four or five, since coats are dear.
On this they were agreed. They didn't fight
About finance. Both partners thought it right
To plan and budget with the greatest care.
They were respectable. They didn't swear.
They disapproved of swearing, and of spending,
Instead of saving, making do and mending.
They disapproved of wild carousing, noise,
And the behaviour of the local boys.

With attitudes and firm opinions this strict,
They frowned upon most people in the district.
And, naturally, they didn't want their boy
To grow up like the local *hoi polloi*.

They trained him to be quiet and obedient,
For his own sake, they said. But it's expedient
For parents who prefer an ordered life
(And such were Mr Skinner and his wife)
To keep their offspring under tight restraint
And bid them suffer this without complaint,
And punish them with violence or coldness
For any spontaneity or boldness.
The poor child must believe that he is blessed
With parents who act always for the best
And if they make him wretched, angry, sad,
This merely demonstrates that he is bad.
I don't believe grown-ups should let a child
Make all the rules or run completely wild
Or get its own way with a piercing scream –
There's little to be said for that extreme.
Undisciplined, spoiled children are a pain
And cause a lot of problems, that is plain,
Whereas a young unfortunate like Paul
Won't inconvenience anyone at all.
But when I hear the politicians' song
About the family and right and wrong
And discipline and all of that, I seethe,
Remembering kids who aren't allowed to breathe.
Family life can be a blessing: true
But don't forget the damage it can do.

When Paul was just a baby he was fed
According to the clock. His mother said
'He can't get everything he wants by crying.
It's best to learn that now. He'll soon stop trying.'
When he could talk, requests were often met
With the old saying, 'Those who ask don't get.'

[56]

He learned that wanting, asking were misguided.
He had to wait and see what she decided.
Sometimes his parents liked to give him treats –
Holidays and outings, presents, sweets –
And they expected lots of gratitude
And wouldn't tolerate a sulky mood.
'I don't like the expression on your face,
Young man,' he'd hear, if he betrayed a trace
Of anger. And, since children always need
To trust their parents, mostly he'd succeed
In burying his feelings, so he couldn't
Have negative emotions when he shouldn't.
They told him he was lucky. He suspected
That wasn't true, though he was not neglected
Or dressed in dirty clothes or underfed.
At half past ten his parents were in bed,
Not in a pub or club or bingo hall –
They didn't like that sort of thing at all.
He heard about kids who were left alone
At night when it was dark, all on their own.
His mother thought it dreadful. She was right.
Paul wouldn't want to be alone at night.
And yet he sometimes liked the sound
Of parents who were not always around.

Paul went to school when he was nearly five.
Like other children, when they first arrive,
He felt quite scared, but thought it best his fears
Should be kept hidden. Some kids were in tears
When it was time for Mum to say goodbye
But Paul had learned to act. He didn't cry.

School was a big surprise. Paul thought that you
Sat at a desk and got some work to do
But he was wrong, it seemed. They let you play
And read you different stories every day.
He liked the stories but felt some distress
At seeing other children make a mess
With powder paint. They got it everywhere –
The floor, their clothes, their faces and their hair.
Mum never let him make a mess like that –
She couldn't stand it in her tidy flat.

So many things to do. It was confusing:
Sometimes you had to choose and Paul found
    choosing
Quite difficult. He'd stand and have a look
Then go into a corner with a book.
A timid child, afraid to have a stab
At new activities, afraid to grab
The thing he wanted, he quite liked the times
When everyone sat down for finger rhymes
Or singing songs or learning ABC
From great big charts with pictures, although he
Got bored with that quite soon because he knew it
And didn't want to keep on going through it.
For Paul could learn things quickly, it turned out,
And no one had to be concerned about
His progress in the basic skills. However,
Though she could see that Paul was fairly clever,
His teacher noticed that the little lad
Was often serious, subdued and sad.
And, when she met his parents, she could see
What they were like, and that they might well be
The cause of his unhappiness. She tried

To help the quiet boy who never cried
And felt he always had to get things right.
She helped him see that now and then he might
Try something new and fail. She wouldn't mind.
He learned that he could trust her to be kind.
Some of the other boys were very tough
And naughty. Some girls, too, were pretty rough
But Mrs Moore (that was her name) knew how
To have them understand what she'd allow
And what would make her very, very cross.
They liked her but they knew that she was boss.

On open evening both Paul's parents sat
With Mrs Moore and had a long, long chat.
The teacher had a lot of time to spare
Because there weren't that many parents there.
Some didn't care and many were afraid
Because they felt they hadn't made the grade
At school, and, if their children were the same,
They thought they'd be told off. The Skinners came
To everything. *Good* parents. Lucky lad.
They'd give him hell if his report was bad
In any way at all. 'He's doing well,'
Said Mrs Moore. 'He's come out of his shell
A lot this year, and made good progress, too,
In all the basic skills. No need for you
To worry. And he's learning to have fun,'
She added. Now, that comment on her son
Did not please Mother. She was never sure
About her Paul's beloved Mrs Moore.
Her clothes were slightly odd and not the sort
A teacher ought to wear, the parent thought –
Too 'trendy' for a woman of her age.

[59]

That dreaded adjective was all the rage
And summed up everything the Skinners hated.
'Well, having fun won't get him educated.'
Mrs Moore breathed in. She mustn't get
Into an argument she might regret.
It wouldn't help the boy. She smiled her best.
'His reading and his maths and all the rest
Are excellent. And I am always glad
When pupils tell me that their mum and dad
Have bought them books.' She went on in this vein
A little while. She wished she could explain
All her beliefs about what children need.
She longed to take the couple's hands and plead
With them to be more loving, less severe
But it would do no good. That much was clear.

Perhaps I am too hard on Mum and Dad,
Presenting them as if they're wholly bad.
Some people liked them. Gus would share a joke
With customers and chat with older folk
Whose visit to his shop was all that they
Would have of human company that day.
Left to himself, the father might have been
Less harsh and strict with Paul, and not so keen
To make him an obedient marionette
But he was busy and he mostly let
His other half do things her way. And she,
What can I say? Well, Mrs S. could be
Extremely helpful if someone was ill.
She'd do their shopping, even pay the bill,
If it was small, and have their children round.
The children didn't like this much. They found
They weren't allowed to move. 'Sit there and draw

[60]

And don't drop anything on my clean floor.'
Oh dear. So much for trying to be nice
About this character. It must suffice.

Paul moved on up the school, while Mrs Moore
Stayed with the first year infants, as before.
Though he was sad at leaving her behind,
Some years he had a teacher just as kind
But other years the teacher didn't take
To Paul, since he or she was too opaque
To grasp that being nicely dressed and clean
With interested parents doesn't mean
That everything is easy for a child.
Paul irritated them – so meek and mild,
When they liked kids with spirit. Or they thought
That he was privileged and that they ought
To take care of the disadvantaged kids,
Whose families had really hit the skids,
With dads in prison, dead or gone away,
And mums who had to struggle through each day.
Don't get me wrong. Those children needed all
The help that they could get. But so did Paul.

At ten he was a boy of average height.
Brown hair. Pale face. His build: it wasn't slight
But fairly sturdy, getting on for podgy –
The food he liked was comforting and stodgy.
By now his academic reputation
Was 'Good ability, poor concentration.'
Instead of getting on with things, he'd gaze
Out of the classroom window, in a daze,
Day-dreaming, worrying or feeling sad –
He was an insecure and anxious lad.

[61]

When he made friends, his mother didn't like them.
When he had plans, she did her best to spike them.
She didn't want him going out to play
When he'd been working hard at school all day.
She wished they'd give him homework. That would
   keep
Him occupied until he went to sleep
And make life easier for Dad and Mum.
She sometimes went to school and asked for some.
One teacher fell in line but most refused
And Mrs Skinner wasn't much amused
When Mr Browning said, 'A boy Paul's age
Should have a social life. He's at a stage
When getting on with other boys is bound
To be important to him, and I've found
That schoolwork suffers when a child feels lonely.
I understand your fears and worries, only
I think that, if you'd let him out to play
A little more, the strategy would pay.'
'I'll have to think about it, Mr Browning,'
She said, stood up, and left the classroom, frowning.
Mr Browning didn't think this speech
Would make much difference but his words did reach
Paul's ears, by chance, because he overheard
His mother when she had a quiet word
With Dad about the teacher's point of view.
Young Paul was touched and grateful. Browning
   knew
And understood, it seemed. He almost cried
To think that there was someone on his side.

This Mr Browning, known to Paul as Sir,
Taught fourth year juniors, those who would transfer

[62]

To secondary school next year. At first
He terrified the good kids – and the worst
Restrained themselves as best they could because
They'd heard tall tales about how strict he was.
And he was big - broad shoulders, six feet tall,
And very keen on football, unlike Paul,
But he was OK, Browning, it turned out –
Not every sportsman is a boorish lout.

'Wake up, Paul.' 'Sorry, Sir.' 'Be quiet, Keith.'
He kept them well and truly underneath
His ample thumb but did it with affection.
He liked them all, they knew it, and correction –
'Sit down, Michelle' – was taken in good part.
Once, when the dinner break was due to start,
He kept Paul back. 'A word.' 'Yes, Sir.' He stood
A little nervously. The brotherhood
And all the sisters left the room. Some smiled
And gave a friendly thumbs up as they filed
Past Paul. What had he done? 'It's not a moan,'
Said Mr Browning when they were alone.
'It's not a telling-off. It seems to me
That you've been working harder recently.
Would you agree?' 'I think so. Sir. Er ... yup.'
'And I can see the difference. Keep it up.
Now listen very carefully to what
I'm just about to say, and please do not
Let it go floating out your other ear.
I want you to remember it next year
And after that. OK? You're very bright
And very likeable. Now hold on tight
To that because it's true. Don't let it go.
Your life is sometimes difficult, I know.'

[63]

Paul didn't know quite what to say. He stared
Down at his feet because he hardly dared
To look at Mr Browning, just in case
The tears began to trickle down his face.
He mumbled 'Thank you, Sir'. 'And, by the way,'
The teacher added. 'Careful what you say
To all the others. Smashing bunch of clients –
But they are not all intellectual giants.'
Paul grinned. 'Now, off you go and have your dinner.
And you remember what I said, Paul Skinner.'

The weeks flew past and soon it was July
When all the fourth years had to say goodbye
To Bridge Street School. The comprehensive beckoned –
The daunting Queen Elizabeth the Second –
And most of them were feeling pretty scared
Although not everybody was prepared
To say so. Paul felt lonely and bereft
When he had said his last farewells and left.
He spent the summer lying on his bed
And lost count of the library books he read.
He listened to the radio a bit
But kept the volume very low, lest it
Upset his mother – music with a beat
Affronted her – and had too much to eat.
She wasn't satisfied. 'Paul, any fool
Can read a book,' she said one day. 'And you'll
Get fat and lazy lying there like that.'
He felt like screaming. 'Come and have a chat.'
'No thanks, Mum. Not just now.' *Leave me alone.*
At least let me be quiet on my own.
He couldn't leave the flat without permission.
On his return he faced an inquisition.

She sensed that when he read a book he stole
Into a world beyond her strict control.

One thing they had to do before term started
Was buy his uniform. He trailed, downhearted,
With mother to the shops. She bought him stuff
That looked ridiculous. 'It's big enough
To last a year or two.' He begged. 'Mum, please!
People will laugh at me if I wear these.'
What did she care? 'You don't appreciate
The things I do for you, young man.' 'Yeah. Great,'
Paul muttered darkly. 'What was that you said?'
'Nothing.' He closed his eyes and shook his head.

The dreaded day arrived and Paul got dressed
In his new clothes. His mother was impressed.
'You *do* look smart, dear.' Then she turned to Gus.
'On this first day I think that one of us
Should walk with him to school.' 'Oh, no, Mum. No!'
Her husband acquiesced. 'All right. I'll go.'
They walked together, but not very far.
Gus stopped and said, 'OK, son. Right you are.
I think you know the way to school from here.
Good luck. And not a word to Mum.' 'No fear.
Thanks, Dad. I'll see you later.' Off he ran –
A big boy now, a frightened little man.

Enormous concrete building. Lots of noise.
Long corridors aloud with girls and boys.
Big Bridge Street fourth years now looked small and
    sweet
In their new uniforms, all clean and neat,
And on their best behaviour. Even so,

[65]

Dawn Green and her friend Michelle had a go
About Paul's clothes. 'You ever seen a clown?'
'Watch out. I think his trousers might fall down.'
They giggled. All his fears were coming true.
Please open, ground, so I can fall right through.
But then he saw some more familiar faces
Milling round the desks and finding places
And some said 'Wotcha, Paul' and some said 'Hi'
And Keith said 'Sit here, mate,' and, by and by,
He felt a little better. That first day
The pupils had to learn to find their way
From class to class and Paul got very worried,
More so than most when, late and lost, he hurried
Down corridors, round corners, up more stairs
And into wrong rooms, where he met the stares
Of lots of people who did not expect him.
He vanished, before they could redirect him.
Next day was not much better, nor the next.
The newest boys and girls were still perplexed
By labyrinths of endless corridors
And finding different rooms on different floors.
Some, when they knew the way, pretended not to.
They turned up late and, asked where they had got to,
Said, 'We was lost.' What could the teacher do?
At this stage in the term it could be true.

One Tuesday, on his way to Drama, Paul
Bumped into Keith and Wayne outside the Hall.
' 'Ey, Paulie, 'ere a minute.' That was Keith.
They took him to a corner underneath
A staircase, whispered 'You like Drama?' 'No.'
He hated it. He didn't want to go.
You had to throw yourself around and yell,

Express your feelings. Paul did not do well.
'Be late with us. It's OK. It's a laugh.
You'll only have to do the second half.'

They liked him, Keith and Wayne. He'd noticed that
In Mr Browning's class. They'd stop and chat
And have a laugh with him and call him 'Mate'.
Sometimes he made them laugh, and that was great.
But this was different. Paul felt pretty scared.
Bunk off part of Drama? If he dared,
He wouldn't have to roll around the floor
Or stretch his arms and stamp his feet and roar,
Or not for forty minutes, anyway.
And he liked Wayne and Keith. Why not? 'OK.'
'Right. Follow me. This way,' said Keith. 'Stay cool.'
He sauntered confidently through the school
And through a door, across the playground to
The outdoor toilets. Paul was in a stew
Already, filled with terror and regret.
Keith calmly offered him a cigarette.
Paul shook his head. 'No thanks.' *Oh God*, he thought,
We're in dead trouble now, if we get caught.
Keith lit up, closed his eyes as he inhaled.
Wayne tried to look as cool as him but failed
And had a coughing fit. 'Hold this for me
A minute, Paul. I got to have a pee.'
Paul took it. Suddenly he froze with fear.
Footsteps. An adult voice. 'Right. Out of here.'
Mr Smart, schoolkeeper on the prowl,
Was standing in the doorway with a scowl.
'Put out those fags. Don't leave them on the floor.
I'll take the rest, if you've got any more.'

[67]

The upshot of this serious transgression:
They had to go and make a full confession
To Mr Yates, the deputy, who tore
A strip or two off them and furthermore
Condemned them to detention. 'Four till five
Tomorrow. And make sure that you arrive.'

Paul had to tell his mother. Hell to pay.
She wouldn't speak when he got home next day.
Cold anger for a week. To Paul it seemed
As if she hated him. Some mothers screamed
And yelled at you. His mother's martyred face
And hostile silence kept him in disgrace.
'I'm sorry Mum. I won't skip class again.'
He tried apologising now and then.
It made no difference with Mum or Dad.
'Your mother's disappointed in you, lad,
And so am I.' He waited for the thaw
But he was never quite forgiven for
His escapade or, rather, for the fact
That he had the capacity to act
As if he were a separate human being,
Without his mother knowing or agreeing.

Did things improve as months and years went by?
Did Mrs Skinner change? And did pigs fly?
Paul sulked at home and learned to play the fool
With Wayne and Keith and other boys at school.
He might as well, since nothing but perfection
Would win him Mum's approval and affection.

She tried to crush his spirit but she failed –
The anger and the life in him prevailed.

He was a mixed-up kid – that's no surprise,
A thorough nuisance, in most teachers' eyes,
A silly boy who liked to mess about,
Intelligent – of that there was no doubt,
But not inclined to work. His concentration
Was pretty poor, likewise his motivation.
As for the parents – all the teaching staff
Knew Skinner had a mother-and-a-half
Who fussed, complained and gave them much advice
On how to do their jobs. She wasn't nice
To deal with. Parents do not always see
That treating teachers with hostility
Will never ever help their darling child,
But cause the family to be reviled
And laughed at in the staffroom. Mrs S.
Became a joke, a monster. As you'll guess,
This made some teachers harder on young Paul.
The prejudice did not affect them all
But he had lots of different teachers here,
Yes, nine or ten, and some changed every year.
The nice ones didn't really get to know him
And Wayne and Keith were always there to show him
That comic business or a muttered quip
Could win you warmth, affection, fellowship.
Paul needed that. His friends were all he had.
He couldn't think of Wayne and Keith as bad.

So, when they said it was OK to nick
A few sweets from the shop, or deftly pick
A magazine or two and stuff them under
Your shirt or sweater, he began to wonder.
Now he was old enough to question all
The values Mum and Dad had taught their Paul.

[69]

A boy must be obedient, clean and quiet
And never answer back. Paul didn't buy it.
A boy must share his parents' narrow creed
For they are always right. Paul disagreed,
And he was good and ready to rebel,
Throw out bathwater and the babe as well.
Perhaps it isn't always wrong to take
What isn't yours. 'What difference does it make?
Shopkeepers do all right. They make a profit
And we just knock a small percentage off it.'
Well, that was Keith's view, frequently expressed.
Paul listened, and, at first, he was distressed
But he got used to it. A year or so
Went by before he thought he'd have a go
And, when he did, it wasn't so much greed
As anger that impelled him to the deed.

His mother, every time she was annoyed
By anything he said or did, enjoyed
Announcing that he'd forfeited – again –
His pocket money for the week, and then
She'd add, 'Remember: he who pays the piper
May call the tune.' *You cow,* he thought. *You viper.*
The scene, repeated nearly every week,
Made Paul so furious he dared not speak.
He'd mutter, as he lay awake at night,
'If I become a thief, it serves her right.'

At last, one day, while mooching round a shop,
He reached out for a penny lollipop
And put it in his pocket. No one saw.
Paul Skinner on the wrong side of the law!
Next day a bar of chocolate was his swag,

And then a tin of cola in his bag,
Some nice new pencils. These he showed with pride
To Wayne and Keith, who saw the funny side.
'You nicked them?' 'Yup.' 'Now, Paul, that's very
    wrong,'
Admonished Keith. All three laughed loud and long,
And, for a moment, Paul was close to joy –
He felt as if he was a normal boy.

For several months he got away with it
But he became less careful, bit by bit.
One morning, as he helped himself to tuck,
Inevitably, retribution struck.
The shopkeeper was watching. Paul walked out.
As soon as he had left, he heard a shout,
'Hey you!' He panicked. Should he run or bluff?
He scarpered but he wasn't fast enough.

Back to the shop. The police. To Carter Street,
The local nick, where he would have to meet
His outraged parents. Now that all was lost,
Paul felt entirely calm, as if a frost
Had numbed him, and his head was very clear.
It's happened. There is nothing left to fear.
Cold anger made him brave. *When they arrive,*
I'll just stay calm and quiet. I'll survive.
And what comes after that won't be as bad –
I'd rather face a court than Mum and Dad.

And then a memory came into his head
That made this waiting-time a watershed.
Some words came back to him: 'You're very bright
And very likeable. Now hold on tight

[71]

To that because it's true. Don't let it go.
Your life is sometimes difficult, I know.'
And suddenly he had to fight back tears.
He sat and thought about the Bridge Street years
When he was small and promising and good,
How Mr Browning saw and understood
What he was up against. And Mrs Moore –
She'd liked him, too, when he was only four.
If they knew what was happening to me,
How sad and disappointed they would be.
Recalling all their warmth and kindness now,
Paul saw himself through their eyes, and saw how
His life was going wrong. Yes, he'd been clever.
You wouldn't think so now because he never
Did any work. He only messed about.
He'd gone on stealing till he got found out.
He could go on like this, just wasting time
And drift into a life of petty crime
To spite his parents and to demonstrate
That they were not the masters of his fate.
Would changing now mean he had given in?
Perhaps there was a better way to win.

At last the dreaded moment. Here they were –
Two policemen, followed by his dad and her,
Red-eyed and yet majestic, every inch
The martyred matriarch. Paul didn't flinch
Or hang his head like someone in disgrace,
But sat up straight and looked her in the face.

Throughout the interview, he was polite.
He told the truth. His manner was contrite
When he was speaking to the police. If Mum

[72]

Said anything, he acted deaf and dumb.
He got off with a caution – just fourteen,
A first offender, and a boy who'd been
Brought up by decent, law-abiding folk
And didn't think that all this was a joke.
Paul listened to the caution gravely, then
Vowed silently he'd never steal again.

Back home, it was the silent treatment. Paul
Stayed in his room, not staring at the wall
But working as he'd never worked before.
Next day, he was escorted door to door
By both his parents. When they reached the school,
Heads turned. Paul was aware he looked a fool
But what the hell. He wouldn't let those two
Get in the way of what he had to do.

' 'Ey, Paul! What 'appened?' News of his arrest
Had reached his mates, and they were both impressed
And sympathetic. Paul told them the story
Although he didn't want the kind of glory
That being nicked could bring. Not now. But they
Were still his friends. He added, 'By the way,
I've done some thinking.' 'Did it 'urt your 'ead?'
'I'm going to try and work at school,' Paul said.
Wayne laughed. Keith nodded. 'Not a bad idea,
If you don't die of boredom by next year.'
'Yeah, well, it's risky,' Paul agreed. 'We'll see.'
All day he listened hard – in Geography,
In French, in Maths, and he felt pretty good
When school was over, till he saw what stood
And waited for him with a face like stone.
Then he remembered, with an inward groan,

What he still had to go through. 'Hello, Mum,'
He said politely. 'Nice of you to come.'
'If I were you, young man, I wouldn't dare
To be sarcastic. I'd be too aware
Of all the hurt and trouble I had caused,
And I would hang my head in shame.' She paused
And looked disdainfully and hard at Paul,
Who didn't hang his head, but stood up tall
And walked beside her looking neither sad
Nor happy. 'I've been talking with your dad
And, when he gets home we'll be telling you
What we've decided that we have to do.'

Early that evening the parental team
Outlined their errant offspring's new regime:
No going out alone, no cash to spend –
A stricter house arrest. When would it end?
They didn't say. All much as Paul expected.
He was determined not to look dejected
But listened quietly, his face a mask,
Which egged his angry mother on to ask
'What have you got to say? We haven't yet
Heard anything from you about regret.
You sit there like a dummy. What did we
Do to deserve this, Paul? Can you tell me?'
I could but it won't help. 'Say something, Paul.'
'I'll never break the law again. That's all.'
'And no apology?' Paul sat there, dumb.
I've got an iron curtain round me, Mum
And I don't owe you anything. I'm free
To see things in my own way, to be me.

When Paul was older, he would sometimes cry
To think of that fourteen-year-old. And I
Am almost crying as I picture him
Alone, now, in his room, and know how grim
The next few years will be. He worked at school,
While all around him others played the fool.
It wasn't easy. Wayne and Keith were irked –
Attempting to distract him while he worked,
They couldn't. 'Paul would rather do a graph,'
Said Keith to Wayne one day, 'than have a laugh.'
They fell about. 'That's good. Perhaps you'll be
A poet, Keith.' 'Oh, no. No thanks. Not me.'
Some of the teachers, on the other hand,
Were slow to notice or to understand
The change in Paul. He'd been 'a waste of space',
'A tiresome idiot', 'a hopeless case'
Since entering the school. But others saw
That he was trying harder than before
And gave him the encouragement he needed
And did their best to see that he succeeded
In passing some exams. And all this time,
Paul's quiet self-containment was a crime
In Mother's eyes. He'd slipped from her control.
He had a sense of purpose and a goal
But it was his, not hers. He didn't care
If she approved or not. He wasn't there,
Not really. Now and then she'd have a go
At getting through. He didn't want to know,
Though sometimes he would have a chat with Dad
When she was out. It always made him sad.
It made him long for happy family life –
If only Gus had had a different wife.

But then, of course, Paul wouldn't have been Paul
But someone else, if he'd been born at all.

When he reached sixteen Paul was old enough
To leave both home and school. Those years were
    tough.
An office job, a bedsit, evening classes,
Eventually enough A-level passes
To get to college. Sometimes in the night
He had to tell himself, 'You're very bright,'
And when he felt depressed and all alone
The thought of all the people he had known
Who'd liked him kept him going, helped him find
Some thoughtful, understanding friends, the kind
He needed. Even so, he'd sometimes sink
Into depression – had to see a shrink
For quite a while. That helped. But Paul can see
That life, for him, is never going to be
A piece of cake. He teaches nowadays.
He isn't bad at it. In certain ways
He's very good, especially – you'll have guessed –
With troubled children who have been oppressed
At home. Paul lives alone. He isn't gay.
I think he'll find someone to love one day
Not too far off – it's not for me to rush him.
I hope that his exhausting job won't crush him.
I wish him health and happiness and all
The best that life can bring. God bless you, Paul.